Pray21

Timothy Eldred

PRAY21

© 2007 Christian Endeavor International
Published by Youthmark 2012

Cover and text design by Haily Meyers

ISBN 978-1-935843-23-8

Printed in the United States of America

For information:
christianendeavor.com
youthmark.com

Contents

A Word from Timothy Eldred

It was all I could do not to fail tenth-grade geometry. Tutors and teachers did their best. But I had some kind of mental block, maybe missed some basic concept somewhere in the past.

I got a D.

Minus.

But I got by.

Some questions in life never get answered. But not because they're never asked. Just because of some mental block. Some basic concept missing.

Everything else in my life seemed fine. *Seemed.* Tim had it together. Outgoing. Confident. Successful. Getting by in life. So no one bothered asking the hard questions.

Some questions never get answered because we don't see any reason to ask. If status quo is adequate, why challenge it?

And then there are the questions we're afraid to ask. Afraid of the answers.

Growth begins with good questions. But if the questions never get asked or answered, growth stalls. A lot of people live and die without answers. Getting by.

It's a tragedy to settle for a D-minus in life.

I was thirty-four before someone asked me the question I'd never faced. My mentor asked, "Who are you?"

Silence. He might as easily have asked me to calculate the hypotenuse of a trapezoidal pentagon. He wasn't just requesting my name, title, or least favorite Disney character. And I knew it. I tried bluffing. He caught me. I only needed to answer the question. I had no idea.

When I eventually figured it out, the answer involved some scary soul searching. The kind I'm inviting you to do. In accepting the Pray21 challenge, you're going to hit some hard questions. Maybe you're young. You need to face the *Who are you?* question now, before you waste years pretending. (By the way, if you've placed your faith in Christ, you can know with absolute certainty who you are. You'll see what I mean at the end of the 21 days.)

Or perhaps you're not so young. A long way down the road. Career established, family growing, and maybe still unaware of your identity or purpose.

(You can know who you are, too. Someone should have helped you figure it out long ago.)

We're all asking the same question. It's not too late to find the answer. And when you find yourself, you'll be able to do *all* God made you to do. And have the time of your life doing it.

You have been created for significance and service, called to mission and ministry. Getting by is not an option. Getting by is getting lost.

Over the next 21 days you'll read about people in the Bible who are just like you. Asking questions. Avoiding questions. Oblivious to the questions. People in discovery. Getting beyond just getting by. When you wrestle with their stories, you'll open doors for *your* journey of discovery.

Maybe you'll let God inside your heart, where he can birth his plan for you. Hopefully you'll begin to recognize and respond to his call.

Learn who you are. Then start asking, *What's next?*

Fifteen or fifty-five, you are God's answer to somebody's questions. Take 21 days to launch a life of change—change in yourself, changing your world.

The journey's about to begin.

Any questions?

21 Days of Discovery

Over the next three weeks…

- You're going to take a close look at Jesus. Who is he…really? Is he powerful enough? Smart enough? Loving enough? Why do you need him?

- You're going to take a close look at yourself. Who are *you*? How did God specially design you? Are you valuable? Are you redeemable? What's your potential?

- And you're going consider your purpose in life. What's your mission from God? Will you like it? How will God make sure you can fulfill it? What can you expect along the way?

The Pray21 journey is a team event. Young people and adults, in pairs or groups, should think, talk, and pray together through these 21 days. All ages are vital to victory.

The apostle Paul wrote to a young pastor named Timothy: "Don't let anyone put you down because you're young. Teach believers with your life: by word, by demeanor, by love, by faith, by integrity."1 Most of Jesus' disciples were teens and twenty-somethings when he left them on their own to continue his mission—with his Spirit to guide and strengthen them.

God has always counted on young people to do great things for him. He still does.

But this growth opportunity isn't just for the young. Everyone has to take it personally. No aloof supervisors—just participants, fellow pilgrims. We urge humility, respect, and honesty from all ages. Encouragement and accountability must flow both up and down the age scale. None of us has arrived; all of us need to learn from each other.

Each of the 21 daily Bible readings ("Background Files") is guided by a question Jesus asked. His questions were among his best tools for cutting to the heart of people's real issues. Listen carefully as he asks you these questions.

We've added a few questions of our own ("Brief Debrief"). We encourage you to get a blank notebook and journal your thoughts, prayers, and commitments as you wrestle with each day's challenges. Private journaling is especially important for the days you're on your own, between meetings with your group or partners. Bring your most important questions, insights, and commitments to share when you connect with others.

Each day we offer a suggested prayer ("Secure Channel") for you to use or adapt.

Each day, you'll be challenged to choose one specific application for real life. But you can't possibly make 21 life changes in 21 days. So use the three weekly "Checkpoints" to narrow down to three commitments that especially stand out to you.

Spiritual discovery means eyes, ears, and heart open.

Open to a deeper relationship with your best Friend ever.

Open to forgiveness and healing, learning and growth.

Open to dreaming God's dream.

Open to doing more than you ever thought possible for him.

So much to discover…

Part 1: Believe

You believe in God? Good. Did you know that God believes in you?

God made you just the way he wanted you to be. Sure, maybe you've done things that have offended him, hurt others, and injured yourself. Not good. But that doesn't change the fact that God made you for himself (he really likes you) and for a purpose, a mission in this life. And he believes you can do it...with his help...because he made you that way.

So when does your purpose for living kick in? When do you get to start doing something really important? Will it be when you "grow up"? When you get a degree? When you get married? When you make partner or manager?

None of the above. Your purpose takes effect NOW! It doesn't matter whether you're a teen or an octogenarian. You've already passed Go. You've already collected all the gifting and spiritual resources from God that you need for mission launch. What? You don't have everything you'll need for the whole journey? Don't worry. God will train and supply you on the job. It's part of the "daily bread" Jesus said to pray for.[2]

But the whole venture starts by agreeing with God. He believes in the *you* that he made. You need to believe in that same *you*. Not with sinful pride, but with faith in your Creator and Provider as you step out and live for him.

So tell God, "You're right about me." And don't just tell him. Show him.

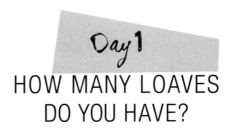

HOW MANY LOAVES DO YOU HAVE?

Got much for God? Me neither. So what does he want from us? Everything. That's all.

What will he do when you bring to him the little that's your everything? He'll multiply it into a feast for thousands. Like he did for Philip. And his other brother Philip.

Read the stories yourself.

BACKGROUND FILES

- Read Mark 6:7–13, 30–45. Might Jesus have been using the food shortage (and his question, verse 38) as a test to see what the disciples learned from their earlier adventures (verses 7–13)?

- Read Mark 8:1–10. Repeat performance! Think about what lesson was so important for Jesus' disciples that he set it up twice.

- Read Acts 8, about a second man named Philip. How did the Lesson of the Loaves apply here?

BRIEF DEBRIEF

These questions are for everyone who follows Christ. Whether fifteen or forty-five, we all frequently need to recommit ourselves and our resources to him. Dig deep and journal about them. Connect with others. Help each other process and pray through the questions and challenges. After you've arrived at some conclusions, continue praying for and supporting each other.

- What tempts you to think that you don't have what it takes to accomplish God's mission? What do you wish you could do for God and others, but are afraid to do? What thoughts and emotions do you wrestle with?

- How many loaves *do* you have? (Be honest.) How might God honor your small-seeming gift?

- What is he asking you to do for him or others this week? Why will this be of value?

- What will you bring to him, for his use?

- What support or resources do you need from others this week? What do they need from you?

SECURE CHANNEL

Lord, when I let myself dream, I get really pumped about all the things I'd like to do for you, and for people. For example…[go ahead, dream with God]…

But I'm usually afraid I don't have what it takes. I hear what you want from me, and I give up before I start. To be honest, I'm afraid you're unrealistic—that you want me to give what I don't even have.

But you promise that that's not true. You just want what I have…everything I have. And as small as that seems to me, here it is. Here I am. As an act of faith in you, this week I will…[commit to one simple, stretching act of obedience]…

I pray these things, too, for [name your partners], that they would courageously give you everything, and that you would provide confidence in your complete sufficiency through them.

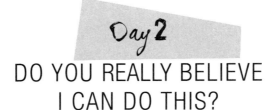
Day 2

DO YOU REALLY BELIEVE I CAN DO THIS?

God wants you to live his dream. But that means taking *him* seriously. How big do you think he really is?

And it means taking *yourself* seriously. Will you dream big with God, and then actively participate in your own dream?

BACKGROUND FILES

- Read Matthew 20:29–34. Think about why Jesus asked these men to state what seemed to be obvious. How was he helping them grow and take a faith risk?

- Read Matthew 9:27–31. Consider Jesus' purpose in asking whether the men were taking him seriously.

- Read Ephesians 3. Look for ways that Paul's dream and God's dream merged into one, guided by God. Paul blows sides off the box in verses 14–21, especially 20–21.

- Read Philippians 3:7–14. Can you hear Paul groaning, trying to express his sold-out passion for the dream?

BRIEF DEBRIEF

Dream about these questions, and journal your thoughts. Think big with a big God (no matter your age or experience). Think and pray big with your partners. Plan together for action.

- "What do you want me to do for you?"[3] What's your dream for God, for changing the world?

- "Do you really believe I can do this?"[4] How big is your God? Big enough for your dream?

- If you haven't already, turn your dream into a request. Step up to the throne and petition the King to make it happen.

- What will be your first step in living the dream?

- Who else do you need to dream and live it with you?

SECURE CHANNEL

Lord, you asked for it. So here's my dream: [Spill it].

There. It's out. Now I choose to see you big, to believe that you can do what I've asked, and even more. Help me trust you, and trust that you made me right for your task. Fill me with true passion for you and your dream.

I pray for all of us [name your partners], that we'd encourage and support each other's dreams, that we'd learn to work in unity for your kingdom.

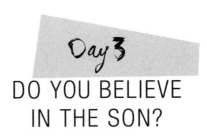

DO YOU BELIEVE IN THE SON?

The miracle life begins with a miracle relationship. Have you become God's son or daughter through Jesus' sacrifice for you? If you have, are you living the passionate miracle life your Father has planned for you?

BACKGROUND FILES

- Read John 9:1–41. What's new in verses 34–38 that hadn't happened before that point? Why could it only happen then, and not before?

- Read Romans 3:20–25. Think about the difference between man's way to "salvation" and God's way. What makes true salvation possible?

- Read Ephesians 2:1–10. Here Paul shows before-and-after snapshots of a person placing faith in Christ. Watch for the hows and how-nots of receiving salvation.

- Read 1 John 5:11–15. Some people think salvation is only a hope, never a certainty. Read what God says.

BRIEF DEBRIEF

Think about these questions, talk with God, and journal about them. When you meet with others, share your thoughts and feelings honestly. Pray together for true knowledge of Jesus, no matter how old you are, and do what you can to help each other find him.

- What's the difference between knowing Jesus and knowing *about* him?

- What's the difference between knowing Jesus and doing the good things he says to do?

- If someone asked you how to start a relationship with Jesus, what would you say?

- Do know the Son of Man? You can pray to him now, using the following prayer or any words that convey the same ideas. Then you'll have his presence in you, helping you live the life you've always really wanted.

SECURE CHANNEL

Jesus, I've done wrong things, and I don't deserve forgiveness or heaven. Thank you for dying for me. I accept your forgiveness, your free gift of eternal life. Change me inside, and help me live for you. Thank you for this miracle *in* me. Now do miracles *through* me.

And if you know Jesus... Lord, thank you for being in my life. Never let me take you for granted. Pull [name your partners] and me closer to you. Let us actually feel like we're starving when we neglect you, so we'll seek you with all our hearts. Live through us and change our world.

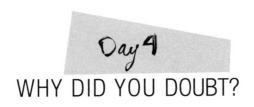

Day 4

WHY DID YOU DOUBT?

God understands our doubts...up to a point. But he loses patience (in love) when we keep hiding in doubts, because he knows how much we can accomplish when we break through and trust him.

BACKGROUND FILES

- Read Matthew 14:22–33. Watch for the things Peter did right and the things he did wrong. Why did Jesus have a right to be disappointed?

- Read the book of Esther, at least chapters 2–4; 5:1–3; chapters 6–8. God isn't mentioned in the story, but his presence and protection is assumed. Keep in mind that Esther was a teenager risking her life to obey God.

- Read Joshua 1:7–9. Joshua was about to attempt the impossible when God gave him this pep talk. Look for ideas for dealing with your doubts about God and your mission.

BRIEF DEBRIEF

Another day, a bigger challenge. Don't face it alone. Connect with your partners soon, and share encouragement, accountability, and prayers. Connect with God about these questions, and journal your responses.

- Describe one doubt that makes it hard for you to trust and obey God.

- What helps you beat it? What makes it worse?

- How do you need people? What can we do for you?

- Don't wait for fear to disappear. Fear isn't the opposite of faith. Disobedience is. What step will you take to show faith in spite of fear this week?

SECURE CHANNEL

Lord, it's hard to admit that I doubt you. I do. [Go ahead. Tell him how you doubt.]

Thanks for understanding. And thanks for not letting me stay stuck. Give me the will to obey, no matter how I feel. And when we've won a victory, let me feel your smile.

I know that [name your partners] are feeling doubts about [fill the blank]. Please give them courage, too.

Day 5

DON'T YOU
KNOW ME YET?

How long have you been with Jesus? Any time with him is time to get to know him. In person.

Open your eyes. He's everywhere in your life. Open your ears. He's talking to you. Open your heart, let him inside. And watch out, world!

BACKGROUND FILES

- Read John 14:1–18. Watch for ways Jesus says we can gain true personal knowledge of God.

- Read Acts 4:13. People couldn't help noticing the transforming power of Jesus' Presence in the lives of these men.

- Read John 15:1–17. Listen to Jesus explaining how to be his friend, as well as some of the results you can expect.

- Read Matthew 25:31–46. Think about the faces in which you "see Jesus" in your daily life, and what he's saying to you when you see him there.

BRIEF DEBRIEF

As you dig into and journal about these questions, picture Jesus there conversing with you. (He really is.) Absorb the love, power, and truth of his Presence. Renew your commitment to seek him each day. Share your commitment with your partners, and prayerfully support each other.

- What are some ways you've seen and come to know Jesus personally in your time with him?

- What difference has this vision of him made in your attitudes and way of living?

- In what ways do you need to open your eyes to Jesus, take a fresh look at him, revive your relationship with him?

- What's one step you'll take now to see and know Jesus better?

SECURE CHANNEL

Jesus, I want to see you. I want the fulfillment of a deep friendship with the God of everything, the central character of all human history. You.

I know I've disappointed you at times, neglecting you, running from you, pretending to be your friend when I've been more like a stranger to you. I'm sorry.

Give me hunger to know you through your Word and prayer. And give me awareness to see your hand and heart in people and events around me.

I pray for the same hunger and sensitivity in my friends, [name your partners].

Part 2: Belong

An amateur once challenged a golf pro to a round...on one condition. The amateur requested two "gotchas." The pro wouldn't admit he didn't know what a gotcha was, so he said okay. The amateur's opening drive was horrible, sliced into a thick grove of trees. The pro teed up, eyed the fairway, and drew back. That's when the amateur dug him in the ribs and yelled, "GOTCHA!"

Later, the other golfers learned that the amateur had won by five strokes. When they asked the pro, all he said was, "You have no idea what it's like playing eighteen holes, waiting for a second gotcha."

We all have gotchas in our past, no matter how long that past is. Trauma, family wounds, painful relationships, sin, failures, labels. We live with ongoing insecurity, waiting for our gotchas to jump up at any moment. They can hinder our relationship with God and our ability to serve him.

If you're a Christ-follower, you confront your gotchas by learning that you *belong*. You were chosen by God to be his forever, and to be part of his mission. You have a secure home waiting in heaven and a church family on earth. You're completely forgiven and accepted. And Jesus is with you through everything.

In these next days, you'll grow more confident in your belonging. But don't wait to launch into your God-given dreams and purpose. He'll use you now!

HAVEN'T I HANDPICKED YOU?

Jesus chose you consciously, with purpose. You weren't forced on him; you weren't his default choice. He wants you. (You have value.) And he has an important mission for you. (You have purpose.) You're handpicked!

BACKGROUND FILES

- Read John 6:66–71. Think about why the Twelve needed the reassurance of verse 70, especially at this point. When do you most need to know God has handpicked you?

- Read Psalm 139. Try to read this as a prayer from your heart to God.

- Read Matthew 10:29–31 and John 3:16–18. How does Jesus speak and show his love for everyone on earth?

- Read Ephesians 1:3–14 or 1 Corinthians 12:4–31. More reasons God has chosen you and made you one of a kind.

BRIEF DEBRIEF

Journal about these questions, continually asking your Father to let you see yourself through his eyes. When you connect with your partners, be God's eyes and voice of love for them, too. Age is not an issue. Everyone needs reassurance.

- What do you honestly believe about your worth to God and your special design for his mission? What are you *told* is true about you, but have a hard time believing?

- What can you do to become more convinced of your value to God?

- What can you do to become more convinced that Jesus wants you on his team, that he has an important job for you to do?

- For today, don't work hard at figuring out what your life assignment is. Focus on simply believing it exists. What's one step you will take toward firmly grasping the truth of your value and purpose?

SECURE CHANNEL

Lord, forgive me for the times I insult you, believing you didn't make me right. Or doubting the power of your grace to clean me up. Or making too little of your amazing love for me.

I go back and forth between thinking too much of myself and thinking too little. (Maybe they're really the same.) Thank you for telling me exactly how you think and feel about me, not leaving me in the dark. Help me believe it. Let it fuel my confident obedience.

Please also show [name your partners] more of your love and your purpose for them. How can I help you answer this prayer in their lives?

WHAT GOOD TO GAIN THE WORLD AND LOSE YOUR SOUL?

Do you ever feel strange in this life? Maybe it's because you're a stranger here. Earth isn't home for God's kids. But you're not a stranger in heaven, your real Home. And you're not a stranger among God's family, your fellow believers. Find strength in these realities to move ahead with your mission on earth, as a friendly foreigner.

BACKGROUND FILES

- Read John 14:1–6. Jesus was about to die when he presented these promises. Last words are lasting words; hang onto them.
- Read 1 Peter 2:9–17. Watch for various reasons we can't get too cozy on earth. How should you live as an alien, rather than a resident?
- Read Mark 8:34–38. Think about the ways these challenges can help Jesus-followers cling more strongly to Home in heaven.

BRIEF DEBRIEF

As you think and journal about these questions, call Home. Talk to your Father about them. And connect with your Homesick brothers and sisters, both older and younger. Talk and pray about this short earthly journey and the long eternity to follow.

- What are the things that tempt you to think of this world as home?
- Even with all the truly good things in this life, why is it dangerous to get too cozy down here?

- What are the possible risks of living as a child of Heaven? Why are they worthwhile?

- What's one new way you need to plug into God's family, your home away from Home?

- What is something on earth that your Father might be asking you to let go of, in order to stand up for him?

SECURE CHANNEL

Lord, thanks for all the gifts you've given me on earth, but help me get in touch with the unbelievably greater gifts in heaven—especially the ones I can have right now. You are the greatest Gift of them all.

To be honest, I think I'm too attached to [something on earth]. I've valued it more highly than you. Help me put things in the right order, you on top. And if that means giving something up, I will. Give me strength to do the right thing.

I pray the same for [name your partners]. Help us relate with each other as your family, helping each other through this earthly journey.

ONE-WEEK
CHECKPOINT

Hey! You've just finished seven days of the Pray21 venture. How're you doing? It is time to stop and take stock.

As we explained in the introduction, it's not humanly possible to actually do a new life application every day. In fact, the way God has designed us, a more realistic life growth pace is one new, deep, lasting life change a month. And that's someone who's really growing. (The way you want to grow, right?)

But these 21 days are different from normal life. They're your special gift to the Lord, meant as a focused time of seeking God's direction—a clarifying, foundation-building endeavor to launch the rest of your life serving him. So everyone participating in Pray21 is planning and praying for an especially concentrated dose of renewed devotion coming out of these three weeks—guided by one personalized commitment from each week.

You might come up with more than three ways you'd like to change, maybe dozens of promises you want to make and keep for the Lord. Write those down! Don't forget them. But for now, just narrow down to three—one each week—that you'll work on for the next couple of months or so.

Starting with this first week...

Think and pray about each of these checkpoint questions, and journal your responses. Meet with your partners to talk and pray together about them, giving each other feedback and encouragement. Participants old and young should seek to learn from God and each other. As you consider this guidance and your own heart passions, choose one key commitment from week one.

1. During the last seven days, what has been the most encouraging, uplifting thought you've had working through this *Discovery Guide*?

2. What has been the hardest idea or challenge for you to swallow? Why do you think this is so hard for you?

3. How have others been helpful to you as you've sought to learn and grow? What more could the rest of us do for you?

4. Have you been able to pray for, encourage, or lovingly challenge one or more of your partners toward growth? If so, describe one way you've done this.

5. Look back over your journaling for these first seven days. Think about the talks you've had with your partners. Does one challenge stand out as God's next step of growth and obedience for you? What is it?

6. **Rubber Meets the Road:** Write down a few details for following through on that next step. For example, what exactly will you do? When? Where? With whom? Who will support you and hold you accountable? How will you know when you've fulfilled your commitment? (Hint: Make your goal stretching and a little risky, but not unrealistic, so you don't just give up.)

7. From these first seven days, what other growth areas, goals, or commitments would you like to pursue some day? Write down a few of those dreams. You can come back to them later.

Day 8

WHAT'S EASIER TO FIX—
BODY OR HEART?

God is a Healer, and he cares about every kind of injury or illness. He's capable of healing any of them, but he's especially concerned about your spiritual injuries—sins—which stand between you and him. These he promises to heal and cleanse absolutely when you ask him to. You can trust that his forgiveness makes you totally acceptable to him.

BACKGROUND FILES

- Read Luke 5:1–32. Jesus performed healing at two levels here, first spiritually (forgiving sin), and then physically. One was invisible, the other visible. God can do both.

- Read 1 John 1:9 and Hebrews 10:17–18. Think about how these promises are important, not only for initial salvation, but for an ongoing close friendship with Jesus.

- Read Isaiah 61:1–3, about the authority and desire of Jesus to heal emotional wounds, like yours.

- Read 2 Corinthians 12:7–10. Why might or might not God heal your physical ailment? What perspective can he give you in either case?

BRIEF DEBRIEF

God promises to forgive all sins when we ask him to.[5] He also heals emotional wounds with time.[6] Sometimes he heals our bodies, sometimes not.[7] Trust his compassion for you as you journal, pray, and connect with your partners.

- Do you have trouble believing in God's complete forgiveness and acceptance of you? If he's forgiven you, have you forgiven yourself, or sought forgiveness from others? Why might these steps be important?

- Is some physical or emotional injury keeping you stuck? If so, explain why. (See also Day 14.)

- Consider your fitness for God's mission. What one specific healing (of sin, emotions, or body) would you request?

- Once you've prayed for this, how can you step out in faith that the Healer has granted it, will grant it over time, or will enable you to live well even with this injury?

SECURE CHANNEL

Lord, I hurt. My spirit sometimes feels dirty. Help me stay close to you through confession, and give me confidence that you forgive and accept me completely. [Tell him specifics.]

You know best how and when to touch my other hurts. I give them all to you. [Tell him what they are.] Heal whatever I need in order to serve you best. Help me obey with patience and joy while enduring any injuries you don't heal, or that take time to heal. I'll be completely whole in heaven, but I can wait...and serve you...until then.

Also bring healing to [name your partners and specific requests for them].

WHO LOVES GOD MORE?

We become trapped by labels that we place on ourselves or accept from others. But no matter what you've done or become, Jesus dismisses the labels when you become his. You can dismiss them, too.

BACKGROUND FILES

- Read Luke 7:36–50. Watch how each character in this story labeled (or didn't) this woman. How did she label herself—before and after? What good were her labels?

- Read Luke 5:1–10. Think about how Peter's label on himself might have hindered his relationship with Jesus, and what he ended up doing about that label.

- Read Matthew 9:9–13, about Jesus confronting labels that the religious hypocrites used to beat people up. How are labels used or abused in Christian circles today?

- Read 1 Timothy 1:12–17. Paul claimed the worst label of all. His point: If God can remove a label like mine, imagine what he can do about yours!

BRIEF DEBRIEF

These questions might challenge you to let go of something you've held dear for years—five years or fifty—something that's hindering you, or killing you. Think, pray, journal, and connect with others. You need help from God and people to release your cherished labels. And people need you.

- What labels do others put on you? Which labels are you most likely to let stick?

- Why do you believe them?

- Is there a difference between a sinful pattern of living and a label? If so, what's the difference? How do their solutions differ?

- If you haven't invited Jesus to forgive your sins, why not now? If you have, but you're still attached to an old label, how can you become convinced the label's a lie? (Truth: You're completely acceptable to your Father.)

- What's your first step?

SECURE CHANNEL

Lord, I've let something outside me define the inside-me. Something false. Something that fools me into thinking you can't love me.

Forgive me...for the sins, but also for the lies I believe about who I really am. I'm your child. I'm a new creation in Christ. I've been genuinely reborn, remade with a new heart. Help me believe it.

[Name your partners] also need to let go of their labels. Please help them experience your forgiveness and your complete acceptance.

WHAT ARE
YOU AFTER?

Knowing Jesus in the flesh was a special privilege for his first disciples. But we now have the greater privilege of having him live *within* us, all the time. Take full advantage of this astounding friendship!

BACKGROUND FILES

- Read John 1:15–51. Think about why the two disciples switched mentors, and what John the Baptist thought about this switch. What drew the disciples to Jesus?

- Read 1 John 1:1. Jesus is a fact, and his Presence makes an impact.

- Read Acts 4:13. What do people see in you when you've been hanging around Jesus?

- Read John 15:1–17. You've already read this passage (Day 5), but read it again. And again. Until you ache for the living Presence of Jesus.

BRIEF DEBRIEF

Dwell in Jesus' Presence as you dig into these questions and journal. Include him in your thoughts, ask him questions, listen. Share your thoughts and plans with your partners, and continue prayerfully supporting each other.

- Have you ever wished you could have been with Jesus in the flesh? How would that have been better?

- What's better about the kind of relationship you can have with him now? Today, how deep can a person's friendship with Christ go?

- What do you do to spend time with Jesus? Does it help you understand him better, or allow you to be more open to him?

- What's something new or something more that you want to do to deepen your friendship with him? What's your first step?

SECURE CHANNEL

Jesus, how well do I really know you? I think if I knew you better, I'd be more and more hungry to connect with you. Because you're the best friend anyone ever had.

I'm sorry for the things and people I've made more important than you in my life. Help me make time for you. I need it. I need you! Change me. And then as I go about my other activities and relationships, make me aware of your Presence all the time.

I pray, too, for your deepening connection with [name your partners]. Pull them closer, and make them more like you.

Part 3:
Become

Have you ever anticipated a growth change in yourself, only to find it wasn't happening nearly as fast as you thought it would? You've probably also had times when you've become so discouraged with your pace of growth that you gave up and thought, *I'm not changing at all.*

The truth is that anyone who's pursuing Jesus and honestly seeking to live for him is changing. No heart that stays focused on him can remain the same. But no one changes completely in a day. Or a week. Or a decade. The life of the most committed, most obedient Jesus-follower is a life of continual learning and growth.

It takes diligence and work, contrary to the common misconception that we simply sit back and let God do it all. And it takes complete dependence on God, contrary to the equally common fallacy that we do it all ourselves. The Godward life is filled with mistakes. And humility. And forgiveness. And risks. And hard times. And strength that increases through hardship.

And the further into this life you go, the more you realize you wouldn't trade it for anything.

Whether you expect your spiritual journey toward eternity to last seven more days or seventy more years, let's look at a few growth dynamics to anticipate as you live a life that counts for Christ.

Day 11

ARE YOU
REALLY LISTENING?

Jesus is speaking all the time, especially to his true followers, in whom he lives. It pays to listen. Really listen. And that means accepting even the hard stuff—his truth is good medicine. Let it change you inside...and outwardly in your living.

BACKGROUND FILES

- Read 1 Samuel 1:20–28; 2:11-36; chapter 3–4, 7. Samuel was a miracle gift to Hannah, who devoted him to God's service. Through-out this story, watch for the contrast between those who listened to God and those who wouldn't.

- Read Mark 4:23–25. Think about what could happen if you really listened to God.

- Read Psalm 19. God speaks with many voices. See how many you can find here. Why so many?

- Read James 1:19–25. What's the harm in "hearing" but not really hearing, "seeing" but not really seeing?

- Optional: Read Isaiah 6:8–10, and consider how it was possible that this tragedy could be true. Have you lived this yourself?

BRIEF DEBRIEF

Speak and listen to God as you work through and journal about these questions. Sometimes God speaks through your partners, so keep your ears open when you connect with them. If you have something encouraging or challeng-ing for them, share it in love. Maybe they need to listen, too.

- How well have you been listening to God lately? What makes listening hard for you?

- Describe one time you listened well, or a time you wish you had listened better. What happened?

- How can you tell the difference between truth from God—through any avenue of communication—and something that's not his truth?

- What is one thing you think God is trying to tell you now?

- How, specifically, will you show him in word and action that you're really listening?

SECURE CHANNEL

Speak, Lord, because I honestly want to hear you. But my "ear"—my heart—gets plugged up with fear, laziness, pride, greed, and more. [Tell him what makes listening hard for you.]

Please change me so I'm more open to you, willing to accept what's hard to accept, and do what's hard to do. I want to talk with you so much and pay such close attention to your truth that you'll always come through loud and clear. Help me trust you so well that I'll obey you without hesitation. This week, to show my love I'll... [tell him your commitment].

I pray the same for [name your partners]. Help them experience the joy of hearing and obeying you without resistance.

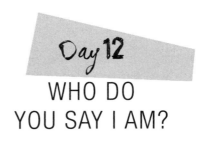
Day 12

WHO DO
YOU SAY I AM?

The world is full of counterfeit christs. If you really want to see the genuine Jesus, he'll show himself to you, and there'll be no mistaking him for one of the imposters. Seek him. Let him be who he really is, not who you wish he was.

BACKGROUND FILES

- Read Matthew 16:13–20. Consider the many different counterfeit christs who want our devotion in today's world. Some are convincing, and some are very similar to the real thing…just different enough to be dangerous.

- Read John 18:1–8. These guys got Jesus' identity partly right…

- Read John 10:1–33. You can learn to recognize the real Shepherd's voice by hanging around with him. Watch how he blows his critics' minds with his real identity (verses 28–33).

- Read 1 John 4:1–8. "Antichrist" literally means "substitute christ," and is used here to describe false human teachers, not the end-times Antichrist. How do you need this warning and reassurance today?

BRIEF DEBRIEF

Meet with Jesus and talk over these questions with him, journaling your thoughts. Help your partners think clearly about Jesus and live for him. Let them help you, too.

- Describe the false jesus who most easily fools you when you let your guard down.

- How is the real Christ different and better?

- Who do you say Jesus is? Choose an answer that zeroes in on the Truth[8] and clearly sets him off from the fakes. Your answer can be as long or short as you need.
- Name one visible difference your Lord will make in your life this week.

SECURE CHANNEL

Jesus, the One and Only, Lord of all lords, I'm deciding now to worship you, only you. I've followed counterfeits before. They don't love me, they've never helped me. Thank you for always being there for me. Thanks for letting me see you.

Teach me discipline to keep my eyes and heart on you. Expose clearly the lies that try to distract me. Protect me. Make me so familiar with your voice that I can't mistake any other voice for yours. And help me show my devotion this week by [tell him one new commitment].

Please also show yourself clearly to [name your partners]. Help them reject the fakes who claim your name.

WHO DOESN'T FIRST FIGURE THE COST?

Talk, but no walk? That's not a disciple. "Gain" without ever any pain? Not a disciple. Squeaking by with minimum investment of self? No dice.

Hand it all over to Jesus—everything you are, everything you have. *That's* a disciple. Once you've done it, you'll never want to live any other way.

BACKGROUND FILES

- Read Luke 14:25–33. Imagine yourself standing in the crowd, hearing these harsh challenges for the first time. Why did Jesus teach this way to a "large crowd" of followers?

- Read Luke 6:43–49, about Jesus' "filters" for separating real disciples from the rest.

- Read Matthew 10, Jesus' training session before sending his disciples out to minister on their own. Do you need this same wake-up call?

BRIEF DEBRIEF

If you take these questions seriously, the outcome could be expensive. And the returns will be beyond your dreams. Journal thoughtfully and prayerfully, and interact with an open heart with your partners, young and old.

- What, if anything, keeps you from selling out to God? Something "better"? Fear of pain or loss? Be specific.

- Brainstorm several benefits of living for God. Consider how much each of them really means.

- Selling out is risky. How does God promise to reimburse, protect, and strengthen you?

- Write your gift list to God. What does "everything" include in your life?

- How you will go about giving him his first gift from your list?

SECURE CHANNEL

(Gulp.) Everything, Lord? And carry a cross to my own execution? This is really tough. The only reason I'm considering it is because of you. Selling out doesn't make total sense to me. But your steady love, your flawless wisdom, your absolute power—these are starting to make sense. And the huge cost is starting to look smaller in comparison to you.

I want to be your disciple. Give me desire to accept the cost. I want to learn to pay it gladly. Show me your hand at work. Give me reassurance and confidence.

And do the same for [name your partners]. Show us how to help each other stay sold out to you.

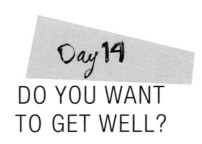

Day 14

DO YOU WANT
TO GET WELL?

We've all be wounded in life. Spiritually, emotionally, physically. At our own hand, by others, and by life's impersonal accidents. God offers healing…restoration to the fully functioning Christ-follower you were always meant to be. But healing sometimes means frightening change, hard work, and pain. It's okay to be afraid, but go ahead…put yourself in the Doctor's care. You can trust him.

BACKGROUND FILES

- Read John 5:1–18. What was Jesus confronting in this man (verse 6)? What other evidence in the passage supports your answer?

- Read John 3:19–21. Think about the reasons that people either seek or avoid spiritual healing (forgiveness and eradication of sin).

- Read 1 Corinthians 1:25–31. Even at our most feeble, how can God use us for his kingdom purposes?

- Read 1 Thessalonians 5:14. Consider how these different instructions apply to people with different attitudes.

BRIEF DEBRIEF

As you wrestle with these questions, be especially honest. With God…with your partners…with yourself. Use your journal as a sounding board. Use your partners as a source of prayer and encouragement. And be the same for them.

- A huge number of people, young and old, have emotional and spiritual illnesses and wounds inside. Pain from abuse, rejection, or neglect. Horrible self-image. Destructive habits and addictions.

Depression... A lot of people prefer to stay sick. Why? What good do they think they're getting out of their condition?

- Do you know someone who doesn't want to get well? Don't mention names. How might Jesus try talking them into accepting his healing?

- How about you? Are you resisting God's healing in some way? Do you know why?

- How might your life be different if you let him make you well?

- What specific steps would lead to your healing? (Consider, for example, prayer, confession, accountability, learning God's truth, getting counseling or rehab.) What do you want to do first?

SECURE CHANNEL

Lord, you've taken care of me in so many ways. [Thank him for specifics.]

But I've held back some of my favorite wounds and sicknesses from your healing touch. I don't completely understand my weird attachment to them. But here they are. [Open them up to him.]

I do want to be well. Completely well. Give me patience with the time it takes. Give me courage for the obedience it takes. Give me humility to be vulnerable and honest. And give me confidence that you still love me, no matter what I dig up inside.

Fix me, so I can know you and serve you better.

[Remember to pray for your partners' complete healing, too.]

TWO-WEEK
CHECKPOINT

The marathon is two-thirds of the way done, just seven more days to go.. Seven more days to go. Let's take a breather and talk about your progress and plans so far.

In Part 1 of your Pray21 venture, you were challenged to *Believe*. To believe in yourself the way God believes in you. To believe in the *you* he made—equipped with the gifts and abilities he has given you, empowered and guided by his presence with you, a child of God, deepening a forever friendship with Jesus. It's true, in yourself you don't have all you need. But when you bring all you have to God, he works miracles through you. *Believe.*

In Part 2, you were reminded that you *Belong*. God wanted you, he chose you, he treasures you, and you're part of his mission. Your real home is heaven, and you'll get there. But during your short stay here on this beautiful, sin-filled planet, no matter what you've done, no matter who you've become, he still wants you. Get right with him as often as it takes, and stay connected with other believers. Get on with the mission. Hang out with Jesus every day. *Belong.*

Now you're well into Part 3, and you're learning what it means to *Become*. To become a mature, complete Christ-follower is to humbly open your ears and heart to God, even for the things you don't want to hear. It's choosing the Christ of the Bible, not the Christ of popular opinion or personal preference. It's giving everything to God, and obeying him in truth, not just in word. It's accepting his healing, taking risks in obedience, and sometimes trusting him even while you're taking some serious hits. All this to *Become.*

- - -

Meet with God and with your partners to work through these checkpoint questions. Be willing to give and receive help and ideas, whether you're younger or older, as you process your commitments together. And record your responses in your journal.

1. How are you feeling at this stage? Tired? Pumped? Scared? Important? Something else? Do you know why?

2. In one or two sentences, how are you now seeing the bigger picture of God's mission for his people on earth?

3. In one or two sentences, summarize your current understanding of God's call for you as a specialist-on-assignment in that mission.

4. How have your partners been helpful to you this week? How have you helped them?

5. Review all you've read, considered, and discussed during this second week (Days 8–14). What is the one new step of growth and obedience you think God wants you to take? It might be brand new for you, or it might be raising the bar on an existing goal. (It might even be one of your "leftover" dream goals from Question 7 in the One-Week Checkpoint.)

6. **Rubber Meets the Road:** Write down the necessary particulars that you need for true follow-through on your commitment. Be sure to include a plan for support and accountability from others. And be sure you have a way of determining whether you're accomplishing your goal. Take a real risk, but keep your commitment real (within your reach to achieve).

7. From Days 8–14, what other growth areas, goals, or commitments would you like to pursue some day? Write them down as reminders for later.

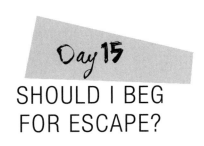

SHOULD I BEG
FOR ESCAPE?

When life knocks you down, take God's sympathetic hand and let him help you up. When you can't get up, he lies down and hurts with you; feel his comfort. And when you think your nightmare is eternal, scream to God and hang onto him; he'll bring morning light in time.

BACKGROUND FILES

- Read Matthew 26:36–56. Try to imagine the hell Jesus was anticipating—about to be cursed by his eternal Father, disowned, smeared with our sin and rejected. Imagine his near-insanity.

- Read John 12:23–33. Jesus powered past his fear by hanging onto his purpose. How can this strategy help you when you're spinning in the middle of a life-tornado?

- Read Job 1:13–22; 2:9–10 (all of chapters 1–2 if you have time). Job lost it all—family, health, everything he owned. He was wretched. But he got past the what and grabbed hold of the Who.

- Read Psalms 42–43. Notice the past joy and anticipated future joy, with despair filling the seemingly endless between. Translate this poet's survival strategy into your own words and life situation.

BRIEF DEBRIEF

Today's questions might stir some frightening memories or worries for you, whether you're young or old. Give yourself a break if you need it. And keep in close touch with someone you trust. (Watch for others, also, who might need to lean on you.)

- Describe a time when you've wished desperately that God, or someone, would rescue you from your pain. (Maybe right now.) How can both honesty about your pain and genuine faith in God work together in those times?

- How long did it take you to heal, if you ever did? What helped? What didn't?

- No one can escape fear and grief when enduring a loss. But brainstorm some ways you can prepare during the easier seasons of life, so you'll hang onto both God and hope when you have to ride out the hard times.

- What's the one step you will take this week to prepare for a future crisis, or to make it through one right now?

SECURE CHANNEL

Lord, when the bottom drops out and I'm in freefall, nothing makes sense. Help me connect closer with you every day, so that in those times at least *you* make sense to me. Teach me to hang onto you no matter what.

Teach me to be completely honest with you. You can handle even my most harsh and despairing thoughts. [If you need to, share your honest thoughts and feelings now.]

Come to me also with silent comfort. [If you're hurting now, you don't have to use words. Just know his presence for a while. Take as long as you need.]

I know, Lord, that [name your partners, if appropriate] are hurting and scared. Let them feel your comfort.

Part 4: Be

It's coming! Some day you'll reach full maturity in Christ. You'll *arrive*, and from that point on you won't need to grow any more. No more struggles to obey. Just keep on walking close to Jesus.

Right?

Right! The day you enter heaven. Meanwhile, perfection is the goal you'll always be approaching, but never reaching in this life.

But that doesn't mean you can't reach a stage called "maturity" while you're down here. In fact, if you give yourself completely to God, you can get there soon. God *wants* you there. You'll be most fulfilled in life when you *get* there. Maturity is the presumed condition for Christ's followers, our natural habitat, the diet on which we thrive. Maturity is supposed to define "normal."

You'll probably discover various plateaus of maturity along your journey, enjoying a season of steady success for Jesus, then discovering another upward growth path. Unfortunately, you may also discover that it's possible to stumble off the edge. And fall a long, long way. Maintaining and enhancing spiritual maturity requires attentiveness and continual dependence on God.

Let's finish the Pray21 venture by learning about a few important principles for life as a mature Jesus-follower.

DIDN'T YOU KNOW I HAD TO BE ABOUT MY FATHER'S BUSINESS?

Whatever your age, your heavenly Father has important work for you to do—kingdom work. Take him seriously. Take yourself seriously. Follow Jesus' example and show yourself to be a faithful, reliable child of your Father.

BACKGROUND FILES

- Read Luke 2, especially verses 39–52, showing both the God-ness and humanness of Jesus. Jesus was one of a kind, but he also lived on earth as our example. Like him, you have your Father's business to manage.

- Read Matthew 5:1–16; 24:42–25:46. What business is the Father entrusting to you? What attitudes are best as you manage it for him?

- Read James 1:27. Why is this an accurate summary of your Father's business? How many churches are majoring on the ministry God considers most important? Is yours? Are you?

BRIEF DEBRIEF

Ready to live and serve like Jesus? Journal your thoughts on these questions, your prayers, your commitments. Share them with your partners, and keep on supporting each other in prayer.

- What are the traditional boundaries limiting the ways "kids" can serve in church? Which of these do you think are biblical boundaries? Which might not be?

- Can you describe one time that you or someone you know served God in an unexpected way—unexpected, maybe, because of age, abilities, personality, background, or some other pigeonhole?
- What is your Father's business?
- How does he want you to be doing it in church? Outside church?
- What's one significant new step you want to take to serve your Father?

SECURE CHANNEL

Father, I'm so glad you adopted me into your family! I love you.

I'm also figuring out that you give your kids chores and household responsibilities. Some of them are fun. Some are hard. Some are dirty. Some are scary. But I want to serve you. Now.

Help me see opportunities for service that I've been overlooking. Help me accept responsibilities I've been avoiding. And if others frown on my service for you, give them insight to guide and encourage me. But give me also respect for the human authorities you've placed in my life.

I pray, too, for [name your partners], that they would give themselves whole-heartedly to your service.

Day 17

WON'T GOD ANSWER HIS CHILDREN'S PERSISTENT PRAYERS?

Praying to an invisible Father, it's sometime hard to believe that he's there, that he cares, and that he listens. Especially when you don't get any response for a long time. But take him at his word. He's there, he cares, he listens, and he will answer your prayer in the very best way and the very best timing. Keep praying.

BACKGROUND FILES

- Read Luke 11:1–13; 18:1–8. In the Bible, repetition means significance. Consider what you're missing if you don't take to heart Jesus' teaching in these two parables.

- Read Ephesians 6:18; Philippians 4:6–7; and 1 Thessalonians 5:17. Prayer was important to Paul. But not just token prayer. Watch for the key words in these passages that describe the most effective kinds of prayer. What might help you genuinely want to pray this way?

BRIEF DEBRIEF

As you journal your responses to the following questions, let the process be a conversation with God. Tell him your thoughts and feelings, and open up to his guidance and love. Open up to your partners, too. Help each other develop more solid and enjoyable prayer habits.

- When you pray, do you think God is listening? Do you think he cares about your requests? Why or why not?

- There are a variety of ways to communicate with God. Take a minute and brainstorm creatively about ways that might work best for you. (Think about all the ways people communicate—speaking, writing, body language, art, music, actions, and more. How might you use these for relating to God?)

- What are a couple of God-honoring desires you want more than anything else?

- What is your strategy for bringing these requests regularly to God? What is your first step?

SECURE CHANNEL

Lord, you're always there. Amazing! And you're better than hanging out with a movie star or sports hero. You can do anything, you know everything, and you never stop loving me. So why don't I connect with you more?

I want to.

I will.

Create in my heart a hunger to be with you. Help me be patient for that hunger to grow, so I don't give up when prayer doesn't come easy.

Do the same thing for [name your partners]. Give them more and more joy in your presence every day.

DO YOU PUT A LAMP UNDER THE BED?

God wants everyone on earth to know him. You're his spotlight, pointing to him, making his heart obvious, unveiling his truth for the world. Shine!

You're also his seed of life, planted on earth. By dying to self, you can take the life he's given you and multiply it hundreds and thousands of times in other people.

BACKGROUND FILES

- Read Matthew 5:14–16. Look around. Think about people and places you encounter. Where might your life-light be helpful? Who might end up thanking you for shining it?

- Read John 12:23–30. Jesus led the way in living out this parable, and he calls you to follow.

- Read Mark 4:1–34. Add the lessons of these farming parables to the one in John 12 above, to understand more fully how you can multiply your life into other lives.

BRIEF DEBRIEF

Here are a few more questions and challenges for you to weigh in your heart—questions and challenges for Christ-followers of all ages. Journal your responses. Process them and pray about them with others, toward personalized commitments and real-life follow-through.

- Think about your life on earth so far. What will you be remembered for when you're gone? What will people say at your funeral?

- What have you contributed to the lives of those around you? How are they different because you lived?

- What's one simple but stretching step you will take this week to shine God's love and truth into the lives of others?

- What has to die in order for this to happen?

- What support or resources do you need from others this week? What do they need from you?

SECURE CHANNEL

Lord, you've given me eternal light and life. What an amazing gift! Thank you.

As grateful as I am, though, I know I've sometimes kept this light to myself, while you want me to shine it and share it. I'm sorry for the opportunities I've missed…the people I've left in the dark. Please forgive me.

I want to start, right now, burning brightly and boldly into the darkness of this world. Give me courage to climb out from under the bed. Help me die to the fear of what others think. Show me how to live as royalty-on-assignment, the child of the King who wants the whole world to be in his family.

I pray this, too, for [name your partners], that they would be able to put to death their self-attitudes, drop the walls, and shine *you* to people around them.

Day 19

DO YOU REALLY LOVE ME?

If you're serious about loving Jesus, he makes it unmistakably clear how he wants us to do it. We love Jesus by loving people. All kinds of people. Even— *especially*—the ones we find least lovable.

Read what God's Word has to say about loving Jesus by loving people.

BACKGROUND FILES

- Read Luke 6:27–38, and ask yourself how some of these familiar phrases can be translated into some unfamiliar actions in your life.

- Read Luke 10:25–37. Remember that the Jews considered the Samaritans to be among the most repulsive of creatures alive. Who are today's equivalents?

- Read John 21:1–17. In verses 15–17, think about the connection between Jesus' questions and his commands to Peter.

BRIEF DEBRIEF

Try to let God's heart fill yours as you consider these questions and journal your responses. Pray for your own inner change, and for change in your partners. Help each other live out a genuine love. We all need help, no matter how old or how accomplished.

- What kind of people do you have the hardest time loving? Why do you think this is?

- Talk about God's attitude toward those same people. Try to get inside his heart and see through his eyes. Try to imagine how he honestly feels toward them. Does it help your attitude?

- What is one opportunity in your daily life to do something kind for an "unlovable" person?

- The mere doing is good and loving, but how can you cultivate a heart that honestly wants to?

- What's your first step?

SECURE CHANNEL

No, Lord, not him. Please don't ask me to love her.

Okay, I've been honest. That's how I feel. (Forgive me.) Now change me. I want to love everyone you love. I want to love the way you love, for the reasons you love. I want to love no matter what.

And I want to love with action. Show me how. Give me courage. Help me get over myself, my fears, and my pride. Help me do miracles in a life that needs you.

Please also help [name your partners] to love all kinds of people in their lives. Fill them with your heart, with your sight, with your touch of healing love.

ARE YOU ABLE TO DRINK FROM THE SAME CUP AS ME?

The privilege of being Jesus' disciple comes bundled together with some responsibilities. Following Jesus means eventually following him all the way to glorious eternity. But between here and there lies the way of the cross. Frightening? Yes. Doable? You bet, with God's help. Worthwhile? Well, let's put it this way: You're not even a disciple if you don't carry your cross.[9]

BACKGROUND FILES

- Read Matthew 20:20–23. The "cup" Jesus referred to was his suffering, and his men knew it. Notice that he took their request seriously, as well as their ability to stomach that bitter cup when the time came.

- Read John 13:1–17. Think about all the ways Jesus is calling you to "wash feet" around you.

- Read Philippians 1:12–21; 2:1–18. What we usually consider highest priorities—safety, liberty, freedom from pain—Paul saw as luxuries. Try to catch his heart in these writings. How can you cultivate the same kind of heart? What's at the center of that heart's devotion?

BRIEF DEBRIEF

Jesus is speaking to followers of all ages and abilities. Listen and share your heart honestly with him and others as you weigh his challenge. Journal your responses to these questions.

- Jesus asks you the question he asked James and John: "Are you able to drink the same cup I drank?" What's your honest answer at this moment? If you're not happy with that answer, what might help you change it?

- Jesus might some day ask you to suffer physically for him. But what are other ways he's likely to ask you to serve and suffer for him?

- What step of service or sacrifice is he asking you to take now?

- How will you start?

SECURE CHANNEL

Lord, I'm scared. But so were you. I guess you understand.

You've promised that your followers will face suffering for your name, but you also promised strength, victory, and great reward.[10] Help me keep my eyes on you, so that any humiliation or sacrifice seems small compared to you.

Also give [name your partners] courage and eagerness to serve and suffer for you.

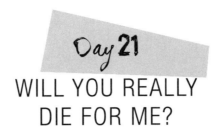

WILL YOU REALLY DIE FOR ME?

What do you do when you've failed Jesus? When you've let him down in a *huge* way? You might be sad and sorry for a while—that's okay. But don't just stay isolated in perpetual mourning. That doesn't do Jesus any good. Let him forgive you, help you back up, and get you back in action. He wants to fix your friendship with him, and he wants you serving in his kingdom.

BACKGROUND FILES

- Read John 13:36–38; 18:1–27. Scene 1: Peter's intentions were good. Have you made promises to God that you might have taken too lightly?

- Read John 21:1–23. Scene 2: Jesus' forgiveness and restoration was complete. Consider how he wants to deal with your failures.

- Read Acts 2:1–47. Scene 3: A repaired instrument can work miracles in God's hand. Don't be afraid to dream about your future, even if you're ashamed of your past or present.

- Read Galatians 2:11–21. Epilogue: Stay alert. You can fall more than once. (And God can help you back up each time.)

BRIEF DEBRIEF

Work through these questions prayerfully with your forgiving, accepting Father. And let your words and prayers with your partners be God's expressions of forgiveness to each other.

- How big a deal does the idea of failing Jesus seem to you? Explain your answer.

- What does Jesus honestly think and feel about the times you fail him?

- What's the way of dealing with your failures that makes Jesus happiest?

- Can you think of a past or present failure that still has you down, out of God's game?

- How will you confront that failure, and get back on with the mission?

SECURE CHANNEL

Lord, when I've failed you, I start to think you don't want me back. I honestly believe, then, that I'm helping you by staying away.

But you tell me you want me back every time. No matter what I've done. Give me honesty to admit my sins and mistakes. Give me strength to accept any negative consequences I've caused. Then show me your unlimited forgiveness—let me honestly believe it. And point me back to the next job you have for me.

Do the same for [name your partners] as they deal with their haunting failures. [Be specific if you can.]

THREE-WEEK CHECKPOINT

In some ways the last three weeks have been a real-life challenge. You've grown, and maybe you've engaged in a spiritual battle or two. You've probably started living out some new principles in your daily life and ministry. That's great. That's real. That's living for God here and now.

But also, in some ways these 21 days have been the conditioning workout for the main event—the rest of your life. You've been making decisions that you still need to put into practice. Clarifying God's game plan for you for the next few months…or years, or decades. Laying some of the blacktop that paves the road to your divine purpose and destiny.

Welcome to the finish line. Welcome to the starting gate.

In Part 4 of your Pray21 venture, you've been challenged to *Be*. To be about your Father's business on earth, now. To be persistent in prayer. To be a light shining in the darkness. To be a lover and caretaker of all kinds of people. To be a servant, and sometimes to be a fellow-sufferer with Christ. To be quick to admit your failures and get back on task for God.

Be.

These are a few of the basics of lifelong, mature commitment to Christ. They're the habits that will help you see your path more clearly as you go. They'll give you the wisdom and stamina and heart to carry out your mission.

And don't forget—*you're on the job now*, even though you may not have finished reading God's job description for you. Take the assignments God sends. Some will come to you, and some you'll need to go find.

And pray. Together and alone. All the time.

- - -

Remember, this exercise is for participants of all ages. We're all on the journey.

Prayerfully plan with God and your partners, looking ahead to the next couple of months. That's the time frame that it may take to establish habitual obedience in the three areas of commitment you're choosing out of this venture. Journal your thoughts as you choose your third goal, as you get ready to launch into Pray22. And Pray23. And Pray24…

1. As best you can right now, finish this sentence: *I think the mission to which God is calling me is…* (Stay open to mission clarification or reassignment later.)

2. What is one specific ministry opportunity you want to pursue as part of this mission? Something you're already doing, or something new? Something boldly visible, or making a difference behind the scenes? Pouring all of yourself into one activity, or touching several causes, each in a significant way? Don't be afraid to dream.

3. From the topics and challenges of this third week (Days 15–21), choose your third new step of growth and obedience. It could be something new, or turning up the dial on a goal you've already been pursuing. Or it might come from your "leftover" dream goals listed under Question 7 in the One-Week or the Two-Week Checkpoints.

4. **Rubber Meets the Road:** Write down your specific plan for follow-through. Will this commitment stretch you? Is it reachable for you? How will you measure success for this goal?

5. **Rubber Meets the Road:** Get out your calendar, schedule it on your mobile calendar, do whatever it takes to jot down some specific dates, times, and places for at least weekly progress check-ins with each other.

6. Write down any other growth areas or commitments from Days 15–21 that you would like to pursue some day. (Idea: Put reminders to yourself in your schedule to look back at these ideas once each month. Regularly reevaluate your current goals, and adjust as needed.)

Remember at the beginning of this book, I said, "If you've placed your faith in Christ, you can know with absolute certainty who you are"? Have you achieved that knowledge? That certainty?

For 21 days you've been on a journey of discovery. You've read. Pondered. Prayed. Talked. Jesus-follower, do you know who you are?

You're a child of the King. Born for greatness. Destined to bring God glory. Your birth Father is the King to whom all other kings, emperors, presidents, and dictators must bow. You have rights. Privileges. He has plans for you. Believe it. Never let go of it.

So what's next? Well, it could be many things. But as you continue with discovery, my final word to you is a warning: Someone wants to rob you. An enemy waits in the wings. You know he's a liar, but he's very good at it. He's looking to confuse you about your identity, to poison your relationship with Jesus.

Stop him at all costs.

Ever since Eden, men and women have battled him. And lost. Relied on mere human logic. Gave up on faith, or never tried it. What birthrights were ours! What a position of honor. All gone.

Great news: What Adam and Eve abandoned, Jesus Christ restored. And, son or daughter of God, that *can't* be taken away from you. Once a prince or princess of heaven, always a prince or princess. You've always been a warrior; now you're assured victory.

The marks of your heritage are permanently tattooed on your heart. Confidence. Courage. Hope. Belief. Faith. Trust. Let them show. These are the Bill of Rights for God's anointed. That's you!

Now, on your enemy's hit list, right next to your name, are your prayer partners. Stay in contact. Remind them of their significance. Replace the words of doubt with God's Word of truth. The truth won't always seem reasonable. What feels right has nothing to do with who you are. Tell each other. Often. Don't let the lies take root.

And dream. With God, many "castles in the sky" are *not* hallucinations. The hope God has placed in you—to change your life and your world—begins when you change your mind. Believe in who you are. Your new, God-transplanted heart knows. Trust its true, deepest confidences.[11] When someone asks you, "Just who do you think you are?"—whip out your ID card: "Child of the King."

For millennia, God has had a task prepared for you. And he's prepared you for the task. He created you with the right raw material, and he's been refining and shaping you. The renovation continues; you're still growing. But it's time to get on with the dream. Chase it down with confident certainty. God is birthing the dream in your heart. And since it's his dream, that means it—or something it's becoming—is destined to come true. You *will* live the dream. Your inner vision will become visible to others on the outside, where God's glory is revealed.

The second-century church father Irenaeus said it well: "The glory of God is man fully alive." Don't let the enemy keep you partly dead. His one purpose is to keep you from fulfilling yours.[12] With Jesus, you'll win.

Your mission, should you choose to accept it, begins now.

And this is one message that will never self-destruct.

(Endnotes)

1   1 Timothy 4:12.

2   See Matthew 6:11.

3   Matthew 20:32, NIV.

4   Matthew 9:28.

5   See 1 John 1:9; Hebrews 10:17–18.

6   See Psalm 34:18; 147:3; Isaiah 61:1–3.

7   See John 9:1–3, 6–7; 2 Corinthians 12:7–10.

8   See John 14:6.

9   See Matthew 10:38.

10   See John 16:33; Matthew 5:10–12; James 1:2–4.

11   "As he thinks within himself, so he is" (Proverbs 23:7, NASB).

12   See John 10:10.